The Vietnam Memorial

CORNERSTONES OF FREEDOM

SECOND SERIES

Sarah De Capua

Children's Press®
A Division of Scholastic Inc.
New York • Toronto • London • Auckland • Sydney
Mexico City • New Delhi • Hong Kong
Danbury, Connecticut

Photographs © 2003: AP/Wide World Photos: 19 (Art Greenspon), 16
(Paul Sakuma), 20 (Schneider), 23, 25, 28, 33, 44 right, 45 left, 45 right
(Charles Tasnadi), 36 (Nick Ut), 13; Corbis Images: cover bottom, 30, 45
center (Bettmann), 35, cover top (Owen Franken), 26 (Catherine Karnow),
3 background, 41 (Joseph Sohm;ChromoSohm Inc.); Getty Images/Alex
Wong/Newsmakers: 31; Hulton|Archive/Getty Images: 14, 15, 21, 38, 39;
Magnum Photos: 10, 44 center (Leonard Freed), 4, 8, 9, 11, 12 (Philip J.
Griffiths), 40 (Peter Marlow), 5, 7 (Marc Riboud); Stockphoto.com/Robert
Ellison: 44 left; Vietnam Veterans Memorial Fund: 32 (Dan Arant), 18, 37.

Dedication: In memory of Corpsman 3.C Ronald R. Reinke

        Library of Congress Cataloging-in-Publication Data
De Capua, Sarah.
  The Vietnam Memorial / Sarah De Capua.
       p. cm. — (Cornerstones of freedom. Second series)
  Summary: A description of the Vietnam Memorial, the memorial which
commemorates the American dead from the Vietnamese Conflict and
which is the most visited monument in the nation's capital.
Includes bibliographical references and index.
  Includes bibliographical references and index.
    ISBN 0-516-24223-7
    1. Vietnam Veterans Memorial (Washington, D.C.)—Juvenile
literature. 2. Washington, D.C.—Buildings, structures, etc.—Juvenile
literature. [1. Vietnam Veterans Memorial (Washington, D.C.) 2. National
monuments. 3. Washington, D.C.—Buildings, structures, etc.] I. Title. II.
Series: Cornerstones of freedom. Second series.
DS559.83.W18D4 2003
959.704'36—dc21

                                                    2003005674

1 2 3 4 5 6 7 8 9 10 R 12 11 10 09 08 07 06 05 04 03

DALE R. BUIS. RAFAEL CRUZ. Leon A. Hunt. Richard Vande Geer. These are just a few of the more than 58,000 names carved on the Vietnam Veterans Memorial. Located in Constitution Gardens on the Mall in Washington, D.C., the memorial is most often called simply the Wall. Since its dedication on November 13, 1982, it has become the most visited **monument** in the nation's capital. A monument is a statue, building, or other work that is meant to remind people of an event or a person. Visitors from all over the world make the Wall one of their first stops in Washington, D.C. There they view the Wall and the two statues that complete the memorial. No matter where they come from, people who visit the Wall are struck by the list of names that goes on and on. The names are those of U.S. service people who were killed or listed as missing during the Vietnam War (1959–1975). The memorial helps people to remember those who lost their lives. It exists to honor the men and women who served their country.

WAR IN A FARAWAY LAND

Prior to the 1950s, many Americans had never heard of Vietnam. Before long, the country came to hold an important place in the history of the United States.

Vietnam is a long, narrow country located in Southeast Asia. It borders the nations of China, Laos, and Cambodia. Beginning in the 1880s, Vietnam was a French **colony**,

A U.S. Marine seeks cover behind his vehicle, while looking for the source of enemy fire in Vietnam, late 1960s.

The suburb of Haiphong in North Vietnam lies in ruins after U.S. bombing in 1969. Despite the military might of the United States, the North Vietnamese and Vietcong were unwavering in their loyalty and commitment to the cause of a united Vietnam.

meaning it was a territory controlled by France. In 1946, unhappy Vietnamese who no longer wanted to be under French control started a rebellion, or armed fight against the government. The rebellion was led by a man named Ho Chi Minh, who was a **Communist**. Communism, in theory, is a system of government that strives for a classless society by eliminating privately owned property and distributing all economic goods equally among people. Its ideals are the

HO CHI MINH

Ho Chi Minh was born in central Vietnam in 1890. When he was twenty-one years old, he left Vietnam to study in France. During this time, he began to follow communism. In 1941, Ho Chi Minh returned to Vietnam and founded a Communist group called the Viet Minh. The Viet Minh fought for Vietnamese independence from France. When the Viet Minh took control of North Vietnam, Ho Chi Minh was named president. He died in 1969. The Viet Minh went on to defeat the non-Communist forces, including the United States, in 1975. Today, the largest city in Vietnam is known as Ho Chi Minh City.

reverse of capitalism, which is the system of government of the United States. Ho Chi Minh and his **guerrilla** army successfully drove out the French, who surrendered, or gave up, in 1954. That same year, the country was divided into two separate nations. North Vietnam was controlled by Ho Chi Minh. It was Communist. South Vietnam was not Communist. The United States supported the non-Communist south.

Elections, processes of choosing leaders by voting, were to be held in 1956 to make Vietnam one country again. However, the leaders of the United States, especially President Dwight D. Eisenhower, were afraid that the Communists would take over all of Vietnam. The United States kept the elections from taking place. U.S. leaders believed if Vietnam became Communist, the governments of the surrounding countries in Southeast Asia could also fall to Communist rebellions. It was in the best interest of the United States to try to contain communism, especially in its standoff with the Soviet Union, which was the world's first and most powerful communist nation at the time. This period of tensions and the race to develop nuclear weapons was called the Cold War. The idea of one country falling to communism causing other countries to do the same was known as the domino theory. As a **democracy**, or country in which government leaders are elected by the people, the United States

opposed communism because it limits people's freedom.
The domino theory was the basis for the U.S. government's
response to the Communist threat.

This photo shows damage resulting from the U.S. bombing of the ancient city of Hue in response to the Tet Offensive. "It became necessary to destroy it in order to save it," was what one U.S. officer said about the destruction in South Vietnam caused by such U.S. efforts.

WOULD VIETNAM BECOME THE NEXT KOREA?

The Korean Peninsula had been divided between the United States and the Soviet Union at the 38th parallel at the start of the Cold War. In 1950, after the last of the U.S. troops had left the newly established Republic of South Korea, Communist North Korea invaded in an attempt to force reunification. The United States then entered and fought against the North. At the beginning of the United States' involvement in Vietnam, many supporters compared it to the Korean Conflict, in which communism had been contained. However, with the Communist movement happening inside South Vietnam, it proved to be a very different war.

As elsewhere in Vietnam, one of the complications facing U.S. forces in Hue was the ability of the enemy to blend in with the civilian population. Here, U.S. soldiers go door-to-door evacuating civilians.

Rebels, people who oppose and fight against a government or ruler, in South Vietnam were called Vietcong. They fought against the South Vietnamese government. The Vietcong were supported by North Vietnam. Their goal was to help the Communist forces defeat the government of South Vietnam so the entire nation would be Communist.

8

As the Vietcong grew stronger, the United States acted. President John F. Kennedy sent 17,000 U.S. troops to South Vietnam between 1962 and 1963. They were sent to help train the army of South Vietnam.

In 1964, it was reported that the North Vietnamese attacked two U.S. ships called destroyers that were off the coast of Vietnam in the Gulf of Tonkin. However, it was later found that President Lyndon B. Johnson manufactured this incident in order to gain the authority he needed to attack North Vietnam. The U.S. **Congress** voted 98–2 to allow President Johnson to take any action necessary to fight the North Vietnamese in what was called the Gulf of Tonkin resolution. Between 1962 and 1975, when the war ended, more than 540,000 American soldiers were sent to Vietnam. Of those, more than 58,000 did not return alive.

PROTESTING THE WAR

As the war in Vietnam dragged on, some Americans began to question U.S. involvement in it. They believed the United States should not be fighting a war in Asia. More-over, some Americans resented that so many young men,

★ ★ ★ ★

This photo shows a demonstration on the Washington Mall against the Vietnam War. These protests increased in size and frequency following the Tet Offensive.

THIRTEEN YEARS

The Vietnam War, in which the United States was involved for thirteen years, was the longest war in U.S. history.

only eighteen to nineteen years of age, were being drafted into the war and killed because the United States did not want all of Vietnam to become Communist.

As more Americans shared this belief, the people of the United States became divided over the war. Millions of Americans believed it was important to support non-Communist South Vietnam. They agreed with the U.S. government position to keep communism from spreading in Southeast Asia. Americans began to argue with each other over what was best for the United States. U.S. military leaders believed the war could be won and asked for more troops to be sent to Vietnam. Many Americans who read newspaper stories and watched television programs of the soldiers fighting and dying, however, thought differently. They believed the war could not be won by the non-Communists. They wanted the United States to get out of Vietnam. One famous proposal was just to declare victory and then leave.

A wounded Marine is assisted by his fellow soldiers in Hue during Tet. The Tet Offensive marked a turning point of the war, as Americans realized that the optimistic reports of U.S. success in Vietnam had been exaggerated in order to win public approval for the continuing war effort.

By the late 1960s, throughout the United States, protests against the war got louder. Protestors gathered in parks, on street corners, and in other public places to **demonstrate**, or join together in protest, against the war. They shouted against the U.S. government and sang peace songs. They

U.S. Marines and Navy corpsmen tend to the wounded in the South Vietnamese city of Hue during the Tet Offensive in early 1968. U.S. forces were surprised by the attack, which coincided with Tet, the Vietnamese festival marking the lunar New Year.

THE DRAFT

The draft is the government selection of men to serve as soldiers. Its official name is the selective service. When young men reach the age of eighteen, they are required to register, or sign up, for the draft. During the Vietnam War, when the U.S. government sent notices to those who were required to report for military duty, many refused to do so. Burning their draft notices was a way to show government leaders that they refused to participate in the war.

A young man burns his draft notice. By 1969, the method for choosing young men to serve in the military was a lottery based on the potential draftee's birthday. Many of those drafted were likely to be assigned to combat duty in Vietnam.

burned American flags, and young men their draft notices. Many times, the protests turned violent.

It was a difficult and confusing time in the United States. Americans were left unhappy and disappointed in their government.

President Richard Nixon uses a television broadcast to explain the expansion of American involvement in the Vietnam War: "If, when the chips are down, the world's most powerful nation, the United States of America, acts like a pitiful, helpless giant, the forces of totalitarianism and anarchy will threaten free nations and free institutions throughout the world."

RETURNING HOME

In 1973, while Richard Nixon was U.S. president, a cease-fire agreement was signed. A cease-fire is an arrangement to end fighting. Most U.S. forces returned home. In April 1975, the Army of North Vietnam ignored the cease-fire and invaded South Vietnam. The South Vietnamese army was quickly defeated. The few remaining U.S. military forces barely escaped being captured by the North Vietnamese. The Communist North Vietnamese had taken over the country. The war was over.

The United States had lost a war for the first time in its history. Many Americans no longer had confidence in the government. They questioned the United States' involvement in Vietnam in the first place. Many thought it would have been just as disastrous if the United States had won.

Returning home to the United States was difficult for Vietnam **veterans**, people who serve in the armed forces, especially during a war. Veterans of earlier wars, particularly World War II (1939–1945), were welcomed home as heroes. Parades were held in their

THE SOCIALIST REPUBLIC OF VIETNAM

Today, Vietnam is still a Communist country. Its official name is the Socialist Republic of Vietnam. Many of its government leaders are the rebels who fought against French then U.S. occupation. More than half of its population of 78 million was born after 1975. This younger generation embraces many American products and trends. Though the older generation is still cautious and distrusting of the United States, to many young Vietnamese the war is "ancient history."

U.S. soldiers in uniform march down Fifth Avenue in New York City during a World War II victory parade. There was no such celebration for those who returned from Vietnam.

A homeless veteran on the streets of San Francisco, California. The treatment of returning veterans by many ordinary Americans made it difficult for those who fought in Vietnam to reenter society successfully. As a result, many suffered from unemployment and homelessness.

honor and government leaders praised them. Families, friends, and even strangers thanked them for serving the country. But this did not happen for the men who returned from Vietnam. Americans were tired of the long war. Many questioned the way the war was fought. They were appalled by the atrocities against Vietnamese civilians. An estimated 3 million civilians died during the Vietnam War. Stories of soldiers' drug abuse, including the use of heroin, had made it back to the United States. When the veterans returned, some were met with **hostility** from people they did not know. Veterans were even spat upon. These feelings were hard for the veterans to accept. After all, by serving in Vietnam they had simply done what their government had ordered of them. Their treatment by many ordinary Americans was unfair and disrespectful. It seemed that everyone in the country—citizens and veterans alike—just wanted to forget about the war.

ONE VETERAN'S DREAM

Jan Scruggs, from Bowie, Maryland, was nineteen years old in 1969 when he decided to join the U.S. Army. He served for more than a year and was wounded. After Scruggs returned home to the United States, he went to college. That is when he first thought about a Vietnam veterans memorial. He believed it was important for Americans to remember the war. He thought a memorial to the men and women who served and died would help the people of the country get over their bad feelings about losing the war.

Jan Scruggs, pictured here, recounted this memory years later about his time in Vietnam: "January 21, 1970, was a typical morning in Vietnam for me. I was serving in Xuan Loc, a town in South Vietnam, with the U.S. Army's 199th Light Infantry Brigade. I had just cleaned an 81-mm mortar and was having coffee. Suddenly there was a deafening explosion. Smoke began billowing about 200 yards away. I ran at full speed and was first on the scene of the disaster. My fellow infantrymen—my friends—were all dead. I was 19 years old, and many of them were no older."

* * * *

Many Vietnam veterans in the United States were having trouble getting their lives back to normal after their experiences in the war. They had seen so much death and destruction. They could not forget the horrors of battle. Some wondered why they survived the war, but their friends had been killed. Many had nightmares and flashbacks, sudden memories of events that were forgotten. There was not much support or compassion from the American public for these veterans and their troubles. Veterans believed there was no one to help them solve their problems. Many became bitter and regretted serving their country. Scruggs hoped that a memorial would help to heal these veterans' broken spirits.

A paratrooper from the 101st Airborne guides a medical evacuation helicopter through the jungle to pick up casualties near Hue in April 1968.

A U.S. marine warns his comrades to keep down as he fires a grenade launcher at North Vietnamese positions. The date is April 19, 1968; he is advancing in order to retrieve the bodies of comrades killed one week earlier.

By 1979, Scruggs was giving much of his time and energy to seeing his dream of a Vietnam veterans memorial become real. He decided that the best kind of memorial would be one that listed the name of every man and woman killed in Vietnam. He told people about his idea. They said it would not work. They believed the country was not ready for a memorial. They thought there were still too many Americans who were angry that the United States had fought in the war. Scruggs did not allow those people to discourage him. He continued to share his idea with anyone who would listen. Eventually, he found people who believed his dream was possible.

With the help of fellow Vietnam veterans Robert Doubek and John Wheeler, Scruggs started the Vietnam Veterans Memorial Fund. This organization developed plans for the memorial. It was also set up to receive **contributions**, or money given to help a person or a project, from citizens and other organizations throughout

For one week in April 1971, Vietnam veterans protested in Washington, D.C., camping out at the Mall and dumping their medals, dog tags, and insignias at the base of the statue of John Marshall, the first great chief justice of the U.S. Supreme Court.

A LITTLE AT A TIME

Much of the $7 million needed to build the memorial came from ordinary Americans. Their contributions came in amounts of $1, $5, $10, and $20 until enough money was raised to pay for the memorial. The rest of the money came from private sources, such as corporations and unions.

the country. At first, however, progress was slow. After one month, the fund had received only $144.50 in contributions. People thought this was proof that no one wanted a Vietnam veterans memorial. Still, Scruggs was not discouraged. He, Doubek, and Wheeler continued to work hard and to ask for contributions. Eventually, over 275,000 Americans contributed a total of $7 million!

Before the memorial could be made, the U.S. **Congress** had to pass a bill giving permission for a memorial to be built in Washington, D.C. Both houses of Congress—the House of Representatives and the Senate—passed the bill unanimously, meaning everyone agreed that the memorial should be built. On July 1, 1980, President Jimmy Carter signed the bill into law. It said that the Vietnam Veterans Memorial would be built on the Mall near the Lincoln Memorial. The Mall is a grassy area lined with trees where people can walk and visit various monuments to important leaders and events in American history. Scruggs was thrilled that the memorial would be built on the Mall, one of the most popular areas of the nation's capital.

The law said a memorial could be built. It did not say what the memorial would look like. That decision was left to the Vietnam Veterans Memorial Fund. However, Scruggs and other leaders of the organization did not know how to design or build memorials. They only knew that they wanted the memorial to draw Americans

Tribute is paid to the fallen soldiers of Vietnam on Veterans Day, November 11, 1986. The seemingly endless list of names on the reflective surface of the Wall always seems to bring visitors closer to the emotional magnitude of the horrors of war.

together. Scruggs also continued to believe that the memorial should contain the name of every man and woman who was killed or listed as missing during the war. Still, they had no idea how this would be done.

THE CONTEST

Scruggs and the other leaders of the Vietnam Veterans Memorial Fund decided to hold a memorial design contest. The contest was open to all Americans. The winner would receive a $20,000 prize and the honor of having his or her design become a permanent part of American history on the Mall in Washington, D.C. There were four guidelines for the entrants to follow: the design should be thought-provoking, compatible with the landscape, include all names of the dead and missing or imprisoned, and not make a political statement about the war.

In October 1980, the Vietnam Veterans Memorial Fund announced the contest to the nation. **Architects** and **sculptors** from throughout the country were especially interested. Competitors were given three months to prepare their designs. By the end of the contest, 1,421 designs were submitted. A group of architects, sculptors, and designers was chosen as judges to pick the winner.

The judges spent one week studying all of the designs. On May 1, 1981, they chose Entry 1,026 as the winner. They called the design "the finest" of all the entries and agreed that it would be an excellent addition to the Mall.

MANY DESIGNS, ONE WINNER

When the memorial designs were spread out for selection by the panel of judges, they filled a large hangar, a building where aircraft are usually kept.

WHO IS MAYA LIN?

Maya Lin is an American whose parents came to the United States from China in the 1940s. Maya was born and raised in the town of Athens, Ohio. A proud American, she was deeply honored when her design was chosen for the Vietnam Veterans Memorial. Since then, she has designed houses and buildings; the Civil Rights Memorial in Montgomery, Alabama; an outdoor chapel in Huntingdon, Pennsylvania; and many other major works. Today, she is considered one of the best public artists in the United States.

Memorial design winner Maya Lin and Jan Scruggs attend a news conference on October 28, 1981, in Washington, D.C. Lin fought for the names on the panels to be listed in chronological rather than alphabetical order so that a visiting veteran could find his time of service within the panel. "It's like a thread of life," she said.

Since its dedication in 1982, the Wall has been the most visited national memorial. More than 40 million people have paid tribute to those fallen in Vietnam. From this view, Maya Lin's vision of the memorial cutting into the earth is evident.

Most people expected the winner to be a well-known architect or sculptor. Everyone was surprised when the winner's name was announced: Maya Ying Lin. No one had ever heard of her. That is because she was not famous. At the time, she was a twenty-one-year-old student at Yale University in Connecticut. She was studying to become an architect. It was not until she won the Vietnam Veterans Memorial design competition that she became famous.

THE WINNING DESIGN

Maya had visited the future site of the memorial before she created her design. Never having experienced the death of a loved one, she wondered how to make her design contemplative about loss and able to help people heal. She later recalled, "[Death and loss] is a sharp pain that lessens with time, but can never quite heal over. . . . I had an impulse to cut open the earth. The grass would grow back but the cut would remain."

A MEMORIAL—AT LAST

On November 13, 1982, the Vietnam Veterans Memorial was dedicated. A crowd of 150,000, mostly Vietnam veterans from all over the country, gathered at the memorial. Jan Scruggs made the announcement he had waited so long to say: "Ladies and gentlemen, the Vietnam Veterans Memorial is now dedicated." Emerging from the earth, the Vietnam Veterans Memorial is a wall shaped like a wide V, made up of two sides, the east wall and the west wall. Each

· GARY D JUDD · TIMOTHY L GILSON · DANIEL W GLEASON · EARNEST W GRAHAM · HERBERT R GRANT
· EDWARD L GRIGGS III · LEE A KEITH · GERALD W GWALTNEY · DONALD W HALLOW · WALTER S HAMNER
· GREGORY E HANKINS · ROOSEVELT HARDY Jr · KENNETH R HEIFNER · LARRY A HARTIGAN · ROBERT W HARTSOCK
· PETE G HECKWINE · NORMAN M HARMON · THOMAS M HIDAY · DOUGLAS L HINKLE · WILLIAM R HODGE
· ROBERT A HORCAJO · CALVIN L HOWELL Jr · JERRY R HOWERTON · NATHAN E HULLETT · GARY E JOHNSON
· KENNETH R JOHNSON · ROBERT L JONES · PHILIP GIGLIO · MARTIN R KEEFE · EDWIN T KEEN
· FREDDIE RAY GUINN · JOHN J KENNEY · ANDREW J KIEFHABER · GREGORY L KOUPE · WOLFRAM J KRETSCHMANN
· KEITH T LANDERS · WILLIAM R LAWSON · JAMES W LEAF · ROBERT M LEE · GREGORY T LINDSAY
· HAROLD S LONERGAN · DENNIS J LORENZINI · ROBERT M LOUGH Jr · LOUIS W MARCIANO · RICHARD S MARK
· JOHN E MARPO · ANDREW M MA   P C MILLER Jr · GARY R MIRACLE
· PAUL J MITCHELL · WILLIAM   D G MOSS · PAUL W MOTLEY
· MICHAEL R McCABE · RONALD McINTO   NANEY · WINFORD A NASS
· FRANK W NELSON Jr · ORLAN M NELSON · DA   · JESSE BARRERA MONTEZ
· JESSE M NUNEZ · JOSE A OLLIVIER ·   BEY · STEPHEN J PASTULA
· GERARD F PAULSEN · JAMES B RIC   NKE   SON · LAWRENCE POET
· DANIEL L POFF · CHRISTOPHER D PRATHER · THOMAS   THOM·   ILLARD F PROCHASKA
· NICHOLAS I PYLE · VICTOR A RABEL · S   ED · JAMI   Jr · MYRON E RHUE
· THEODORE J PAWLOWSKI Jr · CARL J RIEDERER ·   ING · RICH·   FRED L ROACH Jr
· JAY LEE ROBBINS Jr · JON P ROBBINS · HENRY M   Jr · DUANE C K   GE D RUSSELL
· GENE LEO SALZER · RONALD L SANDERS · BOBBY SAN   WILLIAM H SATTER   DEMAKER
· RANDALL F SCHWARTZ · LARRY RAY SHORT ·   HUSTER · SCOTT M   SIDOR
· GEORGE L SILVA · DON   TH · JIMMY V SMITH
· JERRY D SPRAD   TAHL · JERRY W STANBL
· KENNETH E STEINHEBEL · RONA   ON Jr · HENRY R STROB
· RAYMOND SUAREZ Jr · DAVID   EY · ERNEST W SWON
· JO   LOR · DAVID E THA
          ER · JAMES D TYUS
          ADE · WOOTS E WA
          EBER · KELLY W V
          S · CHARLES E W
          C ALDERIDGE ·
          MAS J BURGESO
          C C   ER III

· ERIC T DUFFER · ARTHUR A CROSBY
· JAMES A CRAFT · DAVID A F
· RODNEY M GOODE · JOHN P GRIM
· MICHAEL A HARVEY · DALE
· WENDELL R KELLER · JO
· JOHN W MASSEY Jr · DONALD R MA
· LAWRENCE W PORTER · HEN
· STEVEN R SEGURA · JO
· DOUGLAS J MARKOVICH · BEN H
· JOSEPH L BIDDLE · CHRISTOS C
· ANTHONY B CURCI
· MICHAEL D HYATT · WILLIAM
· DAVID GOMEZ-BADILLO · DAVID L
· RICHARD W KULPA · GEORGE
· THOMAS D THOM
· GORDON L SARGENT Jr · HAR
· RAYMOND E TOLSMA · WALTER B TI
· RAUL ALVARADO Jr · LYT
· BILLY H BEST · GEO
· ROBERT J CAMPBELL · RONA
· HAROLD E CROWDER · JOSEPH H
· CHARLIE FIELDS ·
· RUPERT W GOEBEL Jr · GLEN
· DAVID J PUGLIESI · SAMUEL N HART
· WILLIE J HUDSON ·
· ARLIN W KJO
· WILLIE E MADDEN · LEO J MA
· CALVIN EDMUNDS · DARRYL E M
· JOHN L PRATT · WILLIAM
· WALTER W RUDOLPH · WILL
· JOSEPH SCHMK
· E W THOMPSON · RONA
· LESTER R STO
· A TOMPKINS · RONA
· RED M WILSON · WIL

Making a tracing of the name of a fallen serviceman is a way of bringing a piece of the Wall home, to memorialize the young man who did not return alive.

wall is about 247 feet (75 meters) long. The walls meet at the memorial's highest point, which is 10 feet (3 m) high. The height of each wall gradually decreases to the ends, which are 8 inches (20 centimeters) high.

Each wall is made up of seventy black granite panels on which the names of 58,227 men and eight women are

28

inscribed, or carved. They are listed by date of death or loss. Beside each name is a symbol. A diamond means the person was killed. A cross stands for anyone who was listed by the U.S. military as missing or imprisoned when the war ended. If a person returns alive, a circle will be inscribed around the cross. If the body of an individual is returned, a diamond will be inscribed over the cross.

The first casualties, or people who were killed, occurred in 1959. They are listed on the east wall's first panel. The list of names continues to the east wall's seventieth panel, which ends with May 1968. The names are carried over on the seventieth panel of the west wall. The list continues back to the first panel of the west wall, which is dated 1975. The memorial was designed this way so that the beginning and the end of the war meet in the middle.

CRITICISMS AND COMPROMISES

For the groundbreaking of the memorial to have taken place, the Vietnam Veterans Memorial Fund had to compromise with many Vietnam veterans who rejected Lin's design. Though they had strongly supported the idea of a memorial, when they saw photographs of Lin's design, they had taken back their support. They called the memorial "unheroic" and "a black gash of shame." Others simply called it "ugly."

They thought the use of white marble would make a better-looking monument than black granite. They wanted

CORRECTING MISTAKES

Some names on the Wall were inscribed incorrectly. When this happened, the corrected name was inscribed again, either at the beginning or the end of the same line.

the memorial to be built aboveground instead of buried in the earth. They believed a memorial showing some of the heroism of servicemen and women would be a better way to honor them than a wall. Maya Lin had been disappointed that so many people did not like her design, but she did not change it. "I hope they will give it a chance," she said. *Three Servicemen* and the Vietnam Women's Memorial were added to appease these opponents.

THREE SERVICEMEN

Near the entrance to the memorial site is the lifelike statue called *Three Servicemen*. The 7-foot-high (2-m) bronze statue is the work of sculptor Frederick Hart. The statue's

The unveiling of the *Three Servicemen*. The work is placed so the servicemen appear to be looking at the names on the Wall.

★ ★ ★ ★

The woman pictured here weeps for those friends she knew while serving as a nurse during the Vietnam War. This photo was taken on Memorial Day, 2000.

placement is almost directly across from the Wall. The three young servicemen carry guns, ammunition, and canteens. The statue was dedicated on November 11, 1984.

THE VIETNAM WOMEN'S MEMORIAL

The final piece of the Vietnam Veterans Memorial was dedicated on November 11, 1993. The bronze statue, by sculptor Glenna Goodacre, honors the women of the U.S. Armed Forces who served in the war. The statue shows

WOMEN ON THE WALL

The eight women whose names appear on the Wall are: Eleanor Grace Alexander, Pamela Dorothy Donovan, Carol Ann Elizabeth Drazba, Annie Ruth Graham, Elizabeth Ann Jones, Mary Therese Klinker, Sharon Ann Lane, and Hedwig Diane Orlowski.

31

This woman has come to the Wall to pay tribute to her father on Father's Day. She is a member of an organization of people who lost a father in Vietnam. A Vietnam veteran standing near her can be seen in the reflection on the Wall.

three women helping a wounded soldier. Surrounding the statue are eight yellowwood trees. They symbolize the seven army nurses and one air force nurse who were killed in Vietnam. Their names can be found on the Wall. In all, about 11,500 women served in Vietnam during the war.

VISITING THE VIETNAM VETERANS MEMORIAL

Visitors to the Wall are struck by the number of names and the losses they stand for. People who visit the Wall looking for a specific name have an easy way to find it. A grove of trees stands near the memorial. In this grove are five stands. Each contains a thick book that looks like the telephone directory of a large city. Each book lists the name of every person on the Wall in alphabetical order. Beside each name is the wall panel and line number on which the name can be found.

Once people find the names of those they are looking for, they can make a rubbing of the name. A rubbing is a kind of image, or picture. An information booth near the memorial has paper and pencils available to anyone who wants to make a rubbing. These rubbings are especially meaningful to friends and family members of those on the Wall. It gives them a chance to have a copy of a loved one's name as it appears on the Wall.

HOW TO MAKE A RUBBING

A rubbing is easy to make. Place a piece of paper over a surface that is engraved or has raised letters or images. Hold the paper steady and rub it with a lead or colored pencil, or a crayon. Be sure to hold the pencil or crayon at an angle and rub with the side of the point, not the tip. When you can clearly see the covered image on the paper, you are finished.

33

⋆ ⋆ ⋆ ⋆

OFFERINGS AT THE WALL

Sometimes people leave items along the base of the Wall. Flowers, flags, teddy bears, letters and cards, photos, and medals are among the many different kinds of offerings left at the Wall.

Since the Wall was first being constructed, people have been leaving items at it. In fact, a military service medal lies buried in the concrete beneath the Wall. It was left by the brother of a serviceman killed in Vietnam. The National Park Service oversees the memorial. At first, rangers in the National Park Service did not know what to do with the items. They knew the offerings were meaningful, however, so they did not want to throw them away. Over time, the number of offerings at the Wall grew. The Park Service decided that each item left at the Wall would be kept permanently, like items in a museum. The collection, which today numbers more than 35,000 items, is known as the Vietnam Veterans Memorial Collection. Every night, park rangers collect items left at the Wall during the day. They are taken to a storage building in nearby Lanham, Maryland.

THE WALL THAT HEALS

What should people do if they cannot go to Washington, D.C., to see the Wall? The Wall can go to them!

In 1996, the Vietnam Veterans Memorial Fund introduced a **replica**, an exact copy, of the Wall. It is designed to travel to communities throughout the United States. The

FLOWERS AND FLAGS

Only two kinds of items left at the Wall are not saved: flowers and American flags without messages written on them. Ribbons and messages on the flowers are removed and taken to the storage facility. The flags are donated to the Boy Scouts, Girl Scouts, and other patriotic organizations.

34

Some Vietnam veterans began a tradition of leaving their old combat boots at the Vietnam Memorial in memory of their fallen comrades.

traveling exhibit is called *The Wall That Heals*. It is part of a program known as "Bringing the Wall Home." The program was created as a way for those named on the Wall to "visit" their hometowns and be among friends and family again. The

A Vietnam veteran visits *The Wall That Heals* in Long Beach, California, in 2002. It was the first time the traveling Vietnam Veterans Memorial had appeared in Long Beach. The wall lists over 100 service people from the area who were killed in Vietnam.

traveling exhibit also helps veterans who have been unable or unwilling to visit the Wall in Washington, D.C., to see it in the familiar surroundings of their own communities.

In addition to the replica, the Traveling Museum and Information Center includes exhibits and materials about the Vietnam War,

ONE COMMUNITY'S EXPERIENCE

When *The Wall That Heals* was exhibited in Janesville, Wisconsin, in September 2000, 50,000 people came to view it. Community volunteers took turns reading aloud the names of the 58,220 service people on the Wall. The nonstop reading took fifty-one hours—more than two days—to complete.

In 1999, *The Wall That Heals* made its first international appearance in Ireland to honor the Irish-American casualties of Vietnam.

the memorial, and the service people listed on the Wall.

The Wall That Heals has visited more than one hundred towns and cities throughout the United States. In many communities, ceremonies are held for the family members of those on the Wall.

The exhibit's first international trip took place in April 1999. It was taken to Ireland to honor Irish-born casualties of the Vietnam War and the Irish-Americans who served in the armed forces.

HONOR AND REMEMBRANCE

No one who worked to make the Vietnam Veterans Memorial a reality thought it would become the most visited monument in Washington, D.C. It is more than a monument, however. It is a place where visitors gather to remember the men and women who served their country with honor in Vietnam. There they express gratitude

U.S. soldiers lead captured Vietcong guerrillas onto an army helicopter from a flooded rice paddy in South Vietnam.

A Vietnam veteran visits the Wall on the tenth anniversary of the end of the longest war in American history.

CHARLES J GIBILTERRA Jr • LAWRENCE F GREER • WAYNE D GROAT
DAVID F HEISER • DOUGLAS E HOFFMAN • HOMER W HOLLISTER
GE E JACKSON • RANDALL L JENKINS • CARL R KECK • ASA MARTIN Jr
• LARRY W NEILL • ARTHUR A CALLISTER • RAYMOND NITO RIVERA
ROMERO • PAUL C RUDY • THEODORE M RUSH • RONALD SABIN
• JOHN J SENOR • KENNETH H SHELLEMAN • LEONARD D SMITH Jr
A TRESSLER Jr • JAMES B WHITE • RAY M WILLIAMS • JERRY R DAVIS
N • ISIAH BARNES Jr • RONALD G BAUGHMAN • DONALD C BERRY
LO CASSIDY • THOMAS CLARK • OTIS J DARDEN • ALVIN J DERRICK
ANT • GORDON D GARDNER • GARY LEE GLEAR • DENNIS J GULLA
NSEN • LESLIE A JERSTAD • LESTER JOHNSON Jr • WILLIAM R LARKIN
• MICHAEL S MASSONE • WILLIAM H MILLER • RICKEY C C McCOY
MUSSEN • JOHN R REBITS • ROBERT E SHERLOCK • JAMES E SKIPPER
MPLE • JOHN T WALLS • DENNIS R WHICKER • DAVID R AUGUSTUS
CHAEL A BARNES • ROBERT E BEAUMONT • BENJAMIN H BINEGAR Jr
H H BRUBAKER Jr • LEE E BURNOR • JIMMY O CALL • JAMES D CAMP
S • ANTHONY A BARBARINO • JOHN A DURHAM • ROBERT L EATON
J GILDOW • OTIS GREEN • ANDREW M HAGLAGE • ROBERT K HALL
II • DAVID HOWZE Jr • GREGORY J NICCOLI • ANTHONY A KOSTER
HL • ANTHONY L QUINN • HAROLD R RICHARDSON • JUAN RIVERA
GERALD L THOMAS • HOUSTON F THOMAS • JAMES W TUCK Jr
ALKER • FRANKIE R WILLIAMS • RAY L GOOD • WILLIAM E BOEHM
BURKHART • JAMES L CLARK • LOUIS J CLEVER • JAMES V DORSEY Jr
O • BRUCE B BERNSTEIN • ALVIN GORDON Jr • GERALD J JOHNSON
• GARY R HALEY • ROBERT W HAMLIN • TIMOTHY M HARRINGTON
RD • WILLIAM C. JACKSON • GARY M JOHNSON
ER J KMIT • HOME DONADO-AGUILAR
SKEY • CLARENCE L N NEUBAUER
N Jr • JOHN E NORDEL OLSON
YOR • RUSSELL E REINE RUIS Jr
• JOHN W SPAE GART Jr
• DANA L ZA RISTIANSEN
RRIS • MICH S M KEITH
CHTA • RAFA GDEN
RKER • DON DY
N • TROY CHA
E • RICHA Jr G
BIBEY • G
• ROBER
GARRETT
R JARVIS • G
ELL • RUSSEL
TERSON •

40

to those who fought for freedom. It is a site of deep meaning and importance for the millions of visitors, most of whom never knew anyone whose name is on the Wall, who view it each year. Its permanent place in U.S. history ensures that one hundred years—and more—from now, 58,235 service people who left their families to fight a war and never came home will continue to be remembered.

These names are some of the 58,235 American dead or missing from the war in Vietnam. At its peak, over 200 servicemen a day were killed in action. The estimated number of Vietnamese dead, both military and civilians, is more than 2 million.

Glossary

architects—people who design buildings

colony—a territory that has been settled by people from another country and is controlled by that country

Communist—a follower of communism, which is a system of government that strives for a classless society by eliminating privately owned property and distributing all goods equally among people

compromise—an agreement that is reached after people with opposing views each give up some of their demands

Congress—the government body of the United States that makes laws. Congress is made up of the House of Representatives and the Senate.

contributions—money given to help a person or a project

democracy—a government that has leaders who are elected by the people

demonstrate—to join together with other people to protest something

elections—processes of choosing leaders by voting

guerrilla—a member of a small group of fighters or soldiers that often launches surprise attacks against an official army

hostility—strong hatred or dislike

inscribed—to have carved or engraved letters onto a surface

monument—a statue, building, or other work that is meant to remind people of an event or a person

rebels—people who oppose and fight against a government

replica—an exact copy of something, especially a copy made on a smaller scale than the original

sculptors—people who carve or shape objects out of stone, wood, metal, marble, or clay, or cast in metals such as bronze

veterans—people who have served in the armed forces, especially during a war

Timeline: The Vietnam

1959 1962 1964 1967 1973 1975 1979

1964 The North Vietnamese reportedly attack U.S. destroyers in the Gulf of Tonkin. More U.S. troops are sent to South Vietnam.

1967 U.S. protests against the war get louder as more Americans urge the U.S. government to admit defeat and pull all American troops out of Vietnam.

1973 North Vietnam and South Vietnam agree to a cease-fire.

1975 The Vietnam War ends with the Communist takeover of South Vietnam.

Jan Scruggs devotes much of his time and energy to the establishment of a Vietnam Veterans Memorial.

1959 The Vietnam War begins when Vietcong rebels fight to take over the South Vietnamese government.

1962 President Kennedy sends the first U.S. troops to South Vietnam.

MY SON WAS KILLED! IN VIETNAM WHAT FOR? America

Memorial

JULY
President Jimmy Carter signs the bill into law that will allow the building of a Vietnam Veterans Memorial.

OCTOBER
The Vietnam Veterans Memorial Fund announces the design competition for the Vietnam Veterans Memorial.

Twenty-one-year-old Maya Ying Lin wins the Vietnam Veterans Memorial design competition.

The Vietnam Veterans Memorial is dedicated on November 13.

The *Three Servicemen* statue is dedicated on November 11.

The Friends of the Vietnam Veterans Memorial begins its annual Father's Day ceremony.

The Vietnam Women's Memorial is dedicated on November 11.

The Wall That Heals exhibit is introduced and begins touring the country.

45

To Find Out More

BOOKS

Dubois, Muriel L. *The Vietnam Veterans Memorial*. Mankato, MN: Bridgestone Books, 2002.

Ferry, Joseph. *The Vietnam Veterans Memorial*. Broomall, PA: Mason Crest Publishers, 2002.

Hargrove, Julia. *Vietnam Veterans Memorial*. Carthage, IL: Teaching & Learning Company, 2002.

Yokoe, Lynn. *Maya Lin, Architect*. Parsippany, NJ: Modern Curriculum Press, 1995.

ORGANIZATIONS AND ONLINE SITES

Friends of the Vietnam Veterans Memorial
4200 Wisconsin Avenue NW
Suite 106
Washington, D.C. 20016

The Wall That Heals
http://www.vvmf.org/travelingwall

Vietnam Veterans Memorial—National Park Service
http://www.nps.gov/vive

Index

Bold numbers indicate illustrations.

About the Author

Sarah De Capua received her master of arts in teaching degree in 1993 and has since been educating children, first as a teacher and currently as an editor and author of children's books.

She visited the Vietnam Veterans Memorial for the first time while researching this book. It gave her a new appreciation of the Vietnam War and its effect on the country—especially the friends and families of those who served in the armed forces.

The author is particularly grateful to Deborah Mink, who graciously went above and beyond the call of duty to provide information and, more importantly, the perspective of a family who lost a cherished loved one in Vietnam.

Ms. De Capua has written several books for Children's Press, including *The FBI*, in the Cornerstones of Freedom series. Born and raised in Connecticut, she currently resides in Colorado.